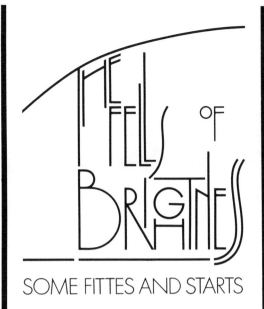

SOME FITTES AND STARTS

Jon Whyte

• Longspoon Press •

Canadian Cataloguing in Publication Data

Whyte, Jon, 1941-
The fells of brightness

Poems.
ISBN 0-919285-18-X

1. Rocky Mountains - Poetry. I. Title.
PS8595.H97F4   C811'.54   C83-091268-1
PR9199.3.W49F4

The Fells of Brightness:Some Fittes and Starts has been set in Univers type.

LONGSPOON PRESS
c/o Dept. of English
University of Alberta
Edmonton, Alberta T6G 2E5

Books may be ordered directly from Longspoon Press or through your bookstore.

Credits:
Editing for the press: *Shirley Neuman*
Book design: *Jorge Frascara*
Typesetting: *Cathy Schmidt*
Printing: *Speedfast, Edmonton*
Financial Assistance: *Alberta Culture*
                    The Canada Council

*for my mother who will not always recognize
"fell," "fitte," and "text" as parts of the fabric,*

but she weaves too

Contents

Preface

The Fells of Brightness, which is to say "Assine Watche," directly translated from Cree, "brilliant mountains," the Rockies; volume I, *Some Fittes and Starts*, which is to say "several cantos and beginnings or surprises." But "fell" is also a folded edge of cloth or textile (which word we derive from the Latin for "text") and "fitte," we find, is a thread weavers used to mark a day's text-making, hence a "hem mark"; and thus "fell" and "fitte" both connote a raised ridge of text, the mountains ranged or arranged.

These notes to get you over the foothills and into the text. I am not purposefully obscure; it would just seem that way. "*The Fells of Brightness*" was a title for an essay on the pioneer Banff photographer Byron Harmon; Oxford found it too rich and called the essay "An Appreciation," freeing it for another use.

The poem's genesis is in my being born and raised in Banff, and in a first leap at a long poem about the Rockies in 1957 when I cast about for a subject big enough for a long poem. I had that year read *Towards the Last Spike* and, if E.J. Pratt could write a poem as long as the CPR, I would write a poem big as a mountain. The Frank Slide was my theme. I knew nothing about it. I've lost or, more likely, thrown away any fragments of that first attempt at epic, but I recall I imitated stout Anglo-Saxon tetrameter. The only line I remember is a description of the mountain about to fall, "like a puma perched upon a pine." Chaucer's parody of alliterative verse in Sir Thopas' Tale trounced such heavy-handed four-point consonance.

I learned English fairly well and crafted poetry variously but, upon returning to Banff in 1968, I began for the first time in a decade to write again about this place. *Homage, Henry Kelsey*[1] intervened, yet one might read it as prologue to *The Fells*, for it incorporates history, myth, landscape, a literary past, and is a foray into "anatomical epic," lying like the prairies before the mountains. Shorter poems—600 to 800 lines; these things are relative—on narratives in Rockies settings[2] were warming-up exercises. In 1977 I began *The Fells* with the assistance of a Canada Council grant. In 1979 I became fully employed and publishers, ever watchful of such goings on, began to request manuscripts. Shirley Neuman, editor of this and my prior book with Longspoon Press, *Gallimaufry*, selected a portion of *The Fells* for inclusion in that book. I have since rewritten that fragment, taking advantage of the typographic realizations I and David Carr had worked out for *Homage, Henry Kelsey* which developed the play of space I had first published in *Open Spaces*,[3] a collection of technopaegnia, concrete, and emblematic poems. That playfulness had since become a liberating breakthrough for me. When Shirley expressed interest in Longspoons's publishing *Some Fittes and Starts*, I noted joyously her having married a book designer in April, 1982, and undertook to rewrite the poem to fulfill a book designer's nightmares.[4] Jorge Frascara, Shirley's husband, became designer for the volume and met several days ago a manuscript meant to invoke the full range of his talents. The results are in your hands. Frequently engaged in book design myself, I tend now to think of "the book," rather than of "the text." To Shirley and Jorge must go a large share of the credit for the realization of *Some Fittes and Starts*.

I forecast now five volumes of *The Fells*, each about the length of this volume, publication to follow leisurely and annually until 1987. *Some Fittes and Starts* is a genesis, establishing the cosmos, and autobiography, providing facts about the neighbourhood and bringing me into awareness; but it is the foundation of my poetics too, plumbing tropes and rhetoric and reestablishing the relevance of the great traditions of English poetry, allowing me the pleasure of bringing together all my love of *epos*, Hopkins, Marianne Moore, Byron, Al Purdy, Wordsworth and wordplay, play, history and old gossip, and folklore and tale. Volume II, "Wenkchemna," will more fully develop themes only suggested here, a sort of "postlapsarian" trope of anisotropism in linguistic, geological and paleozoological terms, starting at the rock barrier which formed Moraine Lake, a result of the *lapsus* of quartzite from a mountain called the Tower of Babel, and then using the ten peaks of the Wenkchemna Range as indices to broadening experience. Volume III, not yet named, starts in Heraclitus and will be fluvial in form. Volume IV, also not yet named, will pick up autobiographical themes, and the ultimate volume, "Summits," will be a sort of *Paradiso*, though I do not suggest life in Banff is *Purgatorio*, or that *Some Fittes and Starts* is *Inferno*.

The concerns of *The Fells* are numerous, but I can perhaps extract a few here to ease your way further into the matter. First is my interest in the form of the *anatomy*, which I prefer to define as "a panoptic treatment of a single subject, or a singular point of view brought to bear on a multiplicity of subjects." Second, and very obvious, is my joy in the richness of English. At one point in "Epeirogeny" I parody the old-fashioned post-modernists; post-modernism was nice while it lasted, I believe. Thank goodness it's over. The language was getting close to atrophying. Third is my dedication to culture and the idea of a cultured person who should, in the late days of the Twentieth Century, be cognizant of Wegener and what J. Tuzo Wilson has done for continental drift, but he should also be aware of Agassiz's contributions to glaciology, and Hutton's and Lyell's more classical geology; additionally he should be aware of the sorts of intelligent mysticism in Paz's *The Monkey Grammarian* (rather than, say, the slick marketing of Carlos Castaneda), the new cosmology of Stephen Hawking, (even if he cannot enunciate much of it), the rigourous imagination brought to bear upon the world by Carl Linnaeus, should have a bending awareness of structural anthropology, and he should be at least blithely aware of popular culture. Coming to the Rockies is not "The Way," but it is certainly among the ways, if only because the Rockies, like mountains everywhere, pose many of the problems of glaciology, geomorphology, ecology, and structuralism. (How did the mountains get carved? How did they get there in the first place? Why is it easier to survey transitions of life forms on a mountain side? Did Lyell and Hutton inform Claude Lévi-Strauss?) Additionally mountains invoke mythology (why did Jehovah talk to Moses on the mountain? Why did Zeus and the gang dwell on Olympus?) and obvious artistic problems (how do we perceive beauty in them in the onslaught of sentimentality?). My Rockies are, I hope, an archetype of anywhere, a complex of folk tale and anecdote, personal experience and Earth, a geography of climate, passion, and place. Should *The Fells* locate my *here*, then perhaps you'll find your *here* both here and everywhere, joyfully and delightfully.

Some illuminations of the book's dark areas I have endeavoured to provide in brief biographies of my kin and neighbours. Since a major segment of "Sources" concerns the Lake Louise region, the interested reader can pursue and peruse the book Carole Harmon and I assembled, *Lake Louise, A Diamond in the Wilderness*.[5] Some of the Whyte (White) family history is recapitulated in *Peter Whyte-Catharine Robb Whyte: A Commemorative Portfolio*,[6] available in some public libraries. *A Hunter of Peace*[7] includes the text of Mary T. S. Schäffer's *Old Indian Trails* and a biography of her by E. J. Hart which omits only one minor fact in her life: my mother visited Mary in 1931, met my father as a consequence of that visit, and ten years later I was a further consequence.

Jon Whyte

December 21, 1982

1   *Homage, Henry Kelsey*, Turnstone Press, Winnipeg, 1981.

2   "Paley" in *Three* (Charles Noble, J.O. Thompson, Jon Whyte), Summerthought, Banff, 1973; "The Agony of Mrs Stone" in *Matrix*, Vol I,1977, Lennoxville, P.Q., "WJP" in *Gallimaufry*, Longspoon Press, Edmonton, 1981.

3   *Open Spaces*, Peter Whyte Gallery, Whyte Foundation, Box 160, Banff, 1977.

4   I note with pleasure that Shirley was a student of mine at the University of Alberta when I taught Creative Writing there, 1966-67. Friends then, nothing has interrupted our affection for each other since. Who is mentor now? Mayhap Shirley.

5   Altitude Publishing, Banff, 1982.

6   Whyte Foundation, Banff, 1980; edited by Jon Whyte.

7   *A Hunter of Peace*, The Whyte Foundation, Banff, 1981.

Sources

The fells:

>high meadows poigned on the spurs of massifs

>mountains   hills   the waste

>fell and dale   summing   summering

In April open

>lowland and fell   to broad and brightening
>
>the barrens   of snow

which   fellfield   brilliant   bears   above

>Sweep back your cape, o fell companion
>let moon light sky   and darken mystery

and

>let the floods of spangling glory dapple
>fell, darkside traveller   time's cosener

>myth   history   family   the contumely

>flood   fell   stone shelves   and cobbles

Fell: all which I feel   find   form   fury
fancy   fantasies   phantoms   phantasms

>all   upon   (which)   my eyes   fall

fell   darkness   fell

>and dreamborne   brilliance   bears

>some streamborne   secret   part
>art
>act
>pact
>past
>fast
>faster

>>forward

Time's augmentation of the space distinguishes
defines
    :lines
    :particularities of aspect
            :distinctions
            :distinction
                  :an inside-
outedness
    making it as special
          as what it limits
so by distinctions
    :mountains define
        :valleys define

    the Fells

:high meadow margins   margins
:hills hemming   hemming
:mountains mooring   mooring
:bens bordering   bordering
:peaks patterning   patterning
:summits summoning   summoning
:Cairngorm loss   loss
    :loss of definition
    :selvage of self

unravelling   ragged   edges   fraying   tailors'   fells

"Take me to a mountain meadow," she dreamt
        spoke
        wrote
    (a clothed softness, like the pleached folds
    (concealing conception upsurgent mountains show;
    (the plaited stems of blossoms on her fingertips
          (entangled)
"and let us dawdle wandering beneath clouds' bellies,
"inspect the spiders' webbings strung from stem to stem;
"I'll ask the flowers' names, and know you know and hope
        "you tell me them;"

(a naked brittleness: the sheer cliffs shorn,
(built to battlement and buttress as scraped
(by vale-deep ice that crept contained by cliff
                                        (and carved them)

"our tongues inspect the honeyed secrets of the blossoms,
"nuzzle and tongue the styles' textures and their sweetness;
"lie, watch clouds play capers on the stony peaks and while
                                        "the afternoon."

(A file of mountains, a rasp of dogteeth pikes
(seen from afar the Sawback seems, the torn horizon:
(will they wear us away? is that what draws us to them
                                        (always?)

Fell: the darkness

and in   my dreams

summing up   it adows me

brevity   succinct summering

alpenglow   and after   stillness

At its shadowed edge
the frayed shore of the dark forest
beside the lake shored
looking at the lake
its farside scene reflected
noting
in the darker parts in nearness
through the surface of the water
toward that which is thither
but the water nearer
the darker, clear bottom of the
lake
the branch-strewn bottom
of the lake
on which a scene is etched
a sketchy scene
and

for a shimmering moment   hold both
eyes   a thriceness   still

lake   reflection   lake bottom

lake   surface   shivers   shimmers

my eyes   fuzz   landscape   blurs

blurring   branches   lin surface   glacier

reflections
and
perceptions

Memory skims the water, a water walker on its surface
walking on its reflection and on the tension brimming
molecule to molecule, force forming film and memory

Four years old
ignorant of lakes
fascinated by the glassbrick
fracturing into repeating parts
the world that enters it
reticulate
each repetition much the same
varying enough by each lens' parallax
to pan
by diffractions
a sort of Eadweard Muybridge vision
of the world

the skeptic amateur of innocence
admires
the rhythm repetition forms and forms

I sway my head with mazy motion
side to side
to bend the world
panoramically around

the mayhem of the terrace
shatters
impossibly into a sort of
order

learning

that which repeats satisfies:

menorah of lodgepole pine; the set meringues of Rundle, Inglismaldie, Goat;
the sharksteeth peaks of Sawback; Ishbel's plates; the ripples on ponds;
the rhymes of Mother Goose, assonance, consonance; mares'-tails, mackerel-sky;
metronomes and pendulums; the pulse points on the carotids; Ravel's *Bolero*;
the wagging of a puppy's tail; dawns and daybreaks; days' similarities;
days' differences; the strata visible on Rundle and Cascade; the echoes;
echoes cusping phrases; phases of the moon; spaced boards of knotty pine;
and patterns of the knots themselves which bodied out the tree;
the lattice of linoleum irregular enough it needed hours and hours to figure out;
telephone pole symmetry, with forty poles marking miles; and railroad ties,
the squares of concrete and the lines distinguishing sidewalks; plaids, setts,
and tartans; lines of fences; lengths of fences; the windows' arches
at the Cave and Basin; the cup hooks in the kitchen cupboard; second hands;
the cyclic path of hours, days, moons, months; and then, as years went by,
the winter-spring-summer-autumn repetition and the sunlight reemergent
over Sulphur; seasons; seasons of years; years; and the ranges' rhythms
started to be apparent too; the great long waves; the waves; the waves

the wave lap   wave lap   wave lap   wave lap   wave lap on the shore

blurred   and   blurring

the thrice held   trice   the trace of

vision's intermingling indistinctions

beyond

the glassbrick window

is the terrace
its flagstone walk, caraganas
borders trimmed with sweet elyssum deer won't eat
larkspur, pale blue and purple, lavender and sky, delphinium
and bumblebeed and hummingbirded
margins of dandelions—poor man's gold—tuffeting
the lawn beside the once-was cabin now garage
and o so neat pineappleweed

(O, I am for those patterns Fibonacciward
(O, O in the order spiraled pineappleweed)

The spruce trees, trees so anciently green
they look as if they've always been there,
been nailed into for corral posts for Peyto's packhorses

> (". . . when Bill Peyto and Jack Sinclair
> ("had the place where your Archives is now . . ."
> (thus Jimmy Simpson, saying it was
> ("the time I saw him make that violin . . ."
> (Jack Sinclair, that is,
> ("went over to Dave White's store
> ("got himself one of those round, wooden cheese boxes . . .
> ("you remember the type of boxes Stilton cheeses used to come in?
> ("Fixed it up and sat down and played it;
> ("had a right good tone, too.")

and I remember reading years later Marianne Moore in "An Octopus"
quoting Walter D. Wilcox's description of Bill Peyto
and realizing, for the first time,
poetry could be about "here" and not "anywhere else,"
and thus could be about "here" and "everywhere else."

Bill Peyto's Cabin: rough-hewn like himself,
placed by the lot's remoter edge, nearer the water,
as far away as he could be and it, yet near enough.
Jack Sinclair packed with Peyto, and prospected;
and when the Boer War came they flipped a coin,
Peyto won the toss and defended the Empire;
while Sinclair stayed in Banff and held the claim,
Peyto rode his horse before the enemy's lines
to draw their fire. After the war was over
Bill came home; and wandering Jack, from Coolgardie
decided to move on and find a fortune in the goldfields
agreeing that my grandfather could buy his lease.
Some five or six years later Jack, who failed to make a fortune,
wrote from an orchard he was working on,
inquiring if his old shack still stood,
and that's the last we hear of Jack
except in Whymper's papers where the cranky Englishman
deplores the actions of his packers, Bill and Jack.

Bill came home and built a legend out of loneliness.
One day he wandered into town and at the butcher's
asked how much a steak two inches thick would cost.
The butcher named a price, and Bill agreed.
Well, after it was cut Bill asked him for some salt
and ate the three-pound slab of meat uncooked.

The Simpsons' place, where Mrs Simpson's sweltering kitchen
havened shortbread on an oilcloth table
and milk to swallow down with tales of Rob Roy:
it was just beyond Big Jim's old midden, or the Mount Royal's,
    (his a rubbish heap, and its a garbage dump);
the ant hill in the rotting stump;
the spruce trees in the loop both bears and brothers climbed;
the lawn, half-mowed by Steve who spoke Ukrainian,
whose hands were mounds, whose rakish fedora always bore a ring of sweat,
    (lawn only to the caragana bush
    (beside the bench which had arrived one Hallowe'en;
    (beyond it was a field of buttercups and wayward asters,
    (marguerites and foxtails, bumblebees and chickadees);
thistles' prickles on the path to Pete'n'Catharine's
which, when running through the hose's spray, were another hazard;
the little tree by our house's corner I knew had grown with me;
the Indian Cabin,
    (it had been Peyto's once but Pete'n'Catharine moved it,
    (moved it from the River Road and settled it
    (where it would block the view of Simpsons',
    (and where the Bearspaws stayed while Pete'n'Catharine
    (painted portraits of them all);
Jack Sinclair's Cabin,
    (moved from Lynx Street down the hill;
    (my father sawed one end out, put in folding doors,
    (making it a garage;
    (before that Quig—Doctor Quigley—
    (lived there a winter, lived in sin,
    (to my very Presbyterian grandmother's deep chagrin);
the carriage shed,
where Perella must have waited patiently for harness,
which Sammy turned into a shop;
near there, and scattered in the spruce,
the elk would lie on winter nights,
their heads like barren branches of leaflorn bushes,
their bodies forming frosty bodyprints in snow;
the chickencoops which demands had turned to flats,
and one of them now held the Packard;

Pete'n'Catharine's home of logs;
and uphill from it where the Stockands lived until the war's end,
when Mildred and the boys moved in
   (and where one day when Billy and I had stolen paint
   (from underneath the Simpsons' porch
   (and swashed the concrete of our house a Kelly green,
   (we fled across the paths and roads
   (and persuaded Mildred we were playing hide'n'seek
   (and hid ourselves beneath the stormdoor basement staircase door);
the spruce tree hedge along both Lynx and Bear that Papa planted,
pruned and thickened to a density forbidding light;
the rose thorn bramble through which the three trails branched:
   to school by way of Mom's yellow stucco bungalow,
   up the ancient river bank where Dietz and Dave had engineered
   a tunnel in the river sand
   that went back sixty feet or more
   and Mom was terrified that one of Ike's cayuses would collapse
   the turf and we'd be buried,
   and we built dams with mud and hauled the hose uphill
   and filled the reservoirs
   into which we'd introduced first ladyfingers
   but building up progressively to blockbusters
   which we'd light and watch the mayhem in the little towns
   we had constructed downstream;
   to overtown from off the driveway,
   past Mrs Simpson's honeysuckles on the corner of their lot;
   and lastly from the porch and up the bank,
   directly past the barbecue of gravity-held bricks,
   (we didn't call it "barbecue," we called it "let's cook outside")
   and by the poplars and the wild roses to the street
   where later, when I was eight, and after Friday Cubs,
   I had to walk to the darkened house,
   and just before I got there,
   only the naked aspen woods to walk down through, but hesitant,
   a rotund bearling ambled out from underneath the compound gate
   and crossed the street and used **our path,**
   and in the darkness I knew he waited and awaited me:

more threatening	dark	it is	to pursue
a threat	into	the	darkness
than to	pursue	mere	darkness

the gravel driveway, source of stones, a glacier-gravel mix
of quartzites, stones with banded calcite,
black stones which gleamed when spat upon,
stones of mauve, deep purple, and rusty quartz,
smooth stones which streams had polished,
rough stones broken into barbs and jaggedness:

scabs	scars	kneepatch	badges
tumbles	falls	accidents	collisions
not wounds	like	Taffy's	scratches

and finally the street, Bear Street,
  (drawn to my attention ultimately
  (it's unusual for streets to have the names of animals;
  (letters came to Bayer, Baher, Baer, and Bare,
  (Behr, and Bier, and Bair, infrequently to Bear)
edged by the spruce of Papa's hedge,
its dark recesses and its secret passageways,
the street.

Beyond	the yard	the place	the street
far beyond	river	stories	relatives
accumulating	density	perception	places
the blurred	background	further	away

the mountains

the Rockies

the world

was never

horizontal:

the hill the ancient river bank provided could impel me into spills,
the driveway's slope provided impetus to wagon rides or sleds,
where we built dams and blew them up we skied at Christmastime,
and where "let's cook outside" was in the undercut we hid,
spring meltwater ran in rivulets to puddle in the loop,
and bicycles scuffed brake marks in the gravel and the dust.

In the stillness

after voices cease

thought's force brims

(meniscus)

into   the temples'   furling   pressure

tension   binding   emotion   skating

as it were

on the bounded undersurface

(surface, however thin, two surfaces still a molecule apart,
(a point thick only, an infinity of points long and wide,
(however long, however wide)

the

infinite

surface

divides

an upperness

a lowerness:

light	ecstatic	circling
essence	ego	rainbow
ascendence	loss	spectre
upwardness	the	myself
convergence	airiness	my
rarefication	of	shadow
integration	pursuit	dancing
atemporality	thematic	in
silence	of	**banked**
greyness	**romantic**	**clouds**
silence	**themes**	**beyond**
time loss	**agony**	**benighting**
disintegration	**in**	**eastern**
chaos	**plunging**	**vault**
divergence	**into**	**as**
downwardness	**pits**	**night**
falling	**of**	**looms**
absolute	**despair**	**gathering**
essence	**falls**	**darkness**

spirits	soul	whiteness
suffusing	silvering	yielding
peaks	transparent	lead
atop	becomes	the
mountains	which	take
far	**slope**	**me**
brilliant	**to**	**beside**
toward	**way**	**ghost**
slopes	**gives**	**pale**
climbing	**ground**	**grim**
exercises	**drops**	**as**
the	**and**	**ghastly**
lank	**valleys**	**fear**
muscles	**seem**	**dragging**
throughout	despondent	gravity
corporeal	thickening	pulling
density	into	relentlessly
into	blackening	shallowing
death	fogs	downwards

Revelation carves from air the puns, the kennings patterns of what carved itself in thought as sculptors translate time and space and make them something solid, the architecture of

Sometimes a thought or quip or joke, a whisper, speech, or utterance, no matter how obvious, apparently conceals beneath itself what it depends upon, the layered awareness of its

I know it seems the usual cliché, but foreshortening suggests at times the whole rough pile of scree will fall upon us, silly as it is to think a

thought as something of a façade, and what we hope is whole but never can quite integrate with memory, the iceberg consciousness that makes our concepts deeper than imagination

dependence on the grottoes, caves, and caverns we in ancient days were lodgers in, the mind's concealments, archetypes, the fire an anodyne to darkness and the cave's bright eye

mountain lacks a foundation and is merely propped up by some sort of false-front brace, and is merely there to hide the struts and gimcracks holding it up

Attend
attenuance
a call to mind
accumulates

Thus: a boundary   of perception

perceiving   and   perceived

membrane thin

(or thick)

less than thin   on the verge

always   ripping

of tearing

letting its contained perceptions

spill

contaminate and flame contagions

spillway   damburst   flashflood   fury

spate and terror

throughout the universe:

so: when voice is silent   manner and style spill

will

never be regained   nor sealed

dispersal's vapours

cloud   accumulate

as in a chilling   the recognitions   cognitions
(anger in danger deserving)
endangered
and deranged   dismembered   torn

and the membrane   meniscus   overbrimmed *it is:*

        not stillness spilled

but is:

        the skin of thought scraped off,
        the raw mind flensed
        as quick blood flows and pale flesh dims

till	all	**the**	lake	surface	**shimmering**	breaks
bottom	branches	**disappear**	**in**	reflected	glacier	**opacity**
reflected	**glacier**	disappears	in	**Monet-**	like	shimmering
only	an	impression	**like**	**glass-**	brick	shattering

                    fell

                the Rockies

bright range: bearing: .

                :story
                :burden
                :the valueless
                :the invaluable
                :the light
                :north
                :by northwest
                :a shining in the west
                :scene and aspect
                :act and motive
                :time, mystery, language
                :recalcitrance
                :force
                :the shape of force
                :silence

                and

lake	:	lake bottom	::	I	:	reflection
(suggestions		(of syllogism				endlessly) reflecting)

			::	brow	:	mind
			::	broken bowl	:	rim
			::	form	:	idea
			::	substance	:	essence
			::	world	:	cosmos
			::	a life	:	a history
			::	a moment	:	eternity
			::	personality	:	humanity

each   analogy   explicating   implicit   analogues   of   surface:

child's mind,   innocence in nature,   the feral and ferocious; so:

five years old,
growing in a sense of tininess
mountains ceasing to be *skena*, the zenith *proskena*

backdrop

Was it then?   At Lake Louise?

(not the postcard Lake Louise, but the place I had not yet been to, seen)

We have continually
to distinguish
occasion of place from place,
and cannot tell
if our first intimations of
infinity
eternity
reflections thereupon
came from within ourselves or
from a first visit to Tommy Armstrong's
barber shop
its mirrors parallel
reflections cannonading into darkening
distance
falling down and bending further down
until I thought that we must disappear
down its long funnel
into the shrinking world
of the Quaker Oats gentlemen
Dutch Cleanser ladies
Mary Jane and Sniffles
(oh, magic words of poof poof piffles)

We have continually
to distinguish
occasion of place from place,
and cannot tell
if our first intimations of
infinity
eternity
reflections thereupon
came from within ourselves or
from a first visit to Tommy Armstrong's
barber shop
its mirrors parallel
reflections cannonading into darkening
distance
falling down and bending further down
until I thought that we must disappear
down its long funnel
into the shrinking world
of the Quaker Oats gentlemen
Dutch Cleanser ladies
Mary Jane and Sniffles
(oh, magic words of poof poof piffles)

We have continually
to distinguish
occasion of place from place,
and cannot tell
if our first intimations of
infinity
eternity
reflections thereupon
came from within ourselves or
from a first visit to Tommy Armstrong's
barber shop
its mirrors parallel
reflections cannonading into darkening
distance
falling down and bending further down
until I thought that we must disappear
down its long funnel
into the shrinking world
of the Quaker Oats gentlemen
Dutch Cleanser ladies
Mary Jane and Sniffles
(oh, magic words of poof poof piffles)

And now I cannot isolate it from the postcard Lake Louise.

Two tour bus drivers, Rocky Mountain Tours boys, students,
roomed with us that summer (one of them Bob Kroetsch's cousin),
took me along for my first mountain climb (mountain? climb?),
Fairview, from the lake's edge by the trail to Saddleback,
and thence from Saddle Col and cabin to the summit cairn.

       How could Walter Wilcox say of Dave White's trail,
       from creek to lake and Saddleback beyond,
       "It is the worst trail I have ever seen"
       when from the fell woods of 1894 there was but it?
       These are sorts of paternosters.

Dark, ancient woods, lichen-hung with Old Man's Beard
and toadstooled, cool, damp, and musty, the rich blush
of swift mountain summer's ripening and rot,
pleat-folded seasons, fell of germination in the duff:
we walked the angling rise of switchbacks upwards,
the way as ancient as the trees, imagining the print
of moccasin in dampened soil, older than trees.

       A first fishing shack by the shore, 1890,
       from trees felled by the lake, Dave White again,
       described its details later on, after his marriage,
       to his father-in-law, John Donaldson Curren,
       so he could paint it, since it had burned down
       in 1891, otherwise quite unrecorded.

Across the avalanche paths, remnants of snow in the thwarts,
emerging to the sun, suddenly our noses sense the differences
of ripening and maturing: what is rotting, what is not,
from the dank, the childhood forest, its toad-world warm and mildew,
to the dry maturing, dusty fronds of grasses, waving in the sun,
tussocks by the boulders where we sat and appled.

       In 1889 George and William Vaux, their sister Mary,
       photographers all three, her demoiselle friend, Mary Sharples,
       (my grandmother's sister's sister-in-law, a "cousin aunt")
       from Philadelphia and Quakers all, rode atop a boxcar
       into steam and wood-ash and a wonder of sensation
       all the way from Morley up to Laggan.

A sorting of the past, a sort of past, sorteeing a past,
and past the marmot-whistled, pika-squealing fellfield,
lichen, tufts of goathair on the rocks' sharp edges,

the last larch far below, and Sheol's bright blackness beckoning,
by zigzags and the trail in dust diminuendoes disappears;
we reach the broad-swept circle of the peaks, the summit.

> The linguist, man of maths, the polymathic Charles Fay,
> the Swiss Guides' "Chipmunk" and climber, Dr. or Professor,
> (somewhere I have a note that shows he also is
> (quite distant kin), was also, 1894, a first precursor
> one who made this slight, albeit meaningful, ascent.

We walk the steps, the trail, the path toward the sky,
while I, an atavist, precede the trail by twenty years
will lead me to an aged unicorn at these bare heights,
a poor old one-horned goat who'll linger here
among the ragged clouds, November cirrus, 1971,
but then in '51 I did not know I walked among the duff
and moulder of the trees that Papa felled, the dust.

It is not the tininess   of the waterskimmers on the lake,
                               ourselves upon the peak's immensity,
                               or the model railroad people at the pass,
but is the hugeness   both of the deepened course of glaciers,
                              and the peaks which ring the blue-cloud tarn,
which suddenly makes time visible   its passage apparent in the cliffs.

Fell of fabric   fold of time

the railroad   pared back

earlier
wandering men
come across the pass
one of them hurt

they hunger   they stumble

in gaunt fear   and   hunger is companion

the Stoneys provide food

dramatis personae are all dead

Years after, seventy or more, Pete and Catharine, painting William Twin:
his eyes closing as he draws pictures from his past,
his mind not dozing.   They ask him questions as they paint:

"Who were . . . who was the first white man you saw? When was that?"

     His wrinkled cheeks,
     his hands' crenellated knuckles,
     mind's mattering battlements,
     iron fell's fells,
     his fingers stretching in the strings of air;
     he puts down the rifle they had borrowed for a prop;
     his picturing place wanders
     from studio to a paintbrush-flowering glen
     William and his twin brother, Joshua, are playing in when
     they meet the strangers, strange white men,
     the first he'd seen.

     His visage innocence becomes
     the ten-year old child he is,
     their camp near where the pipestone is,
         the rivers flow together.

     His there-then mind recalls
     a fragment buried in the soil of change:

         These men come hungry
         from a place
         where people do not go;

         one of them hurts,
         dazed beyond his hunger

     and William sees the man's line pain
     while he reclines against a tree and eats.

Little else:

     he makes the signs:

         pipestone (by mannering its matter)

the rivers merging, "Pipestone" and "Cold-Water River"

an indentation at his brow, his temple

the sunken cheeks

and then:

in quick small taps he pats his head

curls his fingers in a clamp
and clasps his fleshy nose within

looks down

blades his hand at solar plexus

repeats the pats, the clamp of nose.

Passage vanishes.
He sits back again,
his story told.

Pete and Catharine work silently at painting him,
his closing eyes, silent in thought,
inside the story they have seen.

Inside another silence, and leagues remote, another wandering mind:

madness, memory chaotic, maelstrom of speechlessness, confusion
of wapta, washmawapta, waputik, hungabee,
yukness, odaray, opabin and oesa, wiwaxy,
minnestimma, minewakun, and wastach,
the ascension of heejee, nom, yamnee,
tonsa, sapta, shappee, sagowa,
saknowa, neptuak, wenkchemna,
nouns and numbers in Waesgebee
Samuel Allen learned in a summer in paradise
he and others spent near where Twin had met Hector
and placed on the landscape
two years before the mist of madness slunk 'round his mind.

Sam Allen's silence, like Twin's,
pictures without utterance the past.

But then?

"What do you call it?" pointing:
Allen's forefingers point up and away from his temples,
he draws his fingers like dripping rain or dribbling spittle
    down his chin,
stands his two first fingers of his right hand
on his lowered left thumb, and then
prance-capers his slender fingers up the cliffs
    the knuckles form to the little finger's prominence.

And then Twin says, "Waputik."

Allen points to two bright, moving spots of snow,
a faint line across the scree above a cliff, and
"Waputik," he repeats.

Twin smiles and nods, says, "Waputik."

Time is a leaf of gold that does not tarnish,
    a wire of gold drawn fine,
    a ductile line attenuated that ultimately breaks.

Twin scorned Wilcox—"White man no good eyes"
when the white man's fieldglasses revealed but one goat
    and Twin's eyes saw a herd,

but Wilcox praised him:
    "a fine-looking Indian . . .
    "nearer to a realisation of the fine ideal . . .
    "such as one sees on coins . . .
    "than almost any savage's I have ever seen."

Twin   Hector   Vauxes   White   Sharples   Allen   Wilcox   Fay   Whyte

Hector: stumbles near starvation;

Vauxes: photographers all three;

White: builds a log cabin;

Sharples: vows never to sleep in wilderness again;

Allen: learns words and names, goes mad;

Wilcox: subsumes Allen's names and applies his own;

Fay: in the days to come a climber;

Whyte: Peter and Catharine paint William and history recapitulates.

Twin tells Wilcox of his wife, four sons—all dead of smallpox:

"Me sleep no more now
"all time think me
"squaw die, four papooses die
"no sleep me
"one little boy, me
"love little boy, me
"little boy die,
"no longer want to live, me"

And all by which means touch our past

lustre and fanning:

ember   remember

glow   spark   gleam

brighten   against darkness   embodying

flare   glimmering   memory

tinder   into   flame

flicker   the   twigs   to   brilliance

puffs   breath   toward   gathering   warmth

wards   gloom   off   keeps   flames

growing   sticks   hearth   and   heats

mouldering   memories   alive   in   the   minds   of   ourselves   after

the   past   has   started   to   seem   a   chimærical   dance   of   fire

and then

All that is fell   **is brightness**

Geosophy

GAEA   cloaking an emptiness
                  yearning pudendal fulfilment
  GAEA   her mind in her void
                  her energy cleaves
    GAEA   fusing the bursting
                  transmuting primality
      GAEA   into burgeoning
                  collapse, the orgasmic
        GAEA convening of passions
                  in cloacal concealment
         GAEA becoming the mothering
                  dreaming exhaustion
         GAEA mater-materium   URANUS
                  and her passion
          GAEA tunes spheres   URANUS
                  and the background
                  the coldness of space   URANUS
                  while soft rain
                  falls to her clefts   URANUS
                  her hollows and folds
TETHYS   and puddles to ponds **URANUS**
                  to lakes, streams and
  TETHYS   rivers, seas, ocean **URANUS**
                  the coupling of Gaea
    TETHYS   opening gulf and **URANUS**
                  conceiving together
      TETHYS   time and titans
                  the cyclops, the builders
      TETHYS   the mountains
                  the rippling of flesh   EROS
       TETHYS   into chasm and canyon
                  nursing bright water   EROS
       TETHYS the glistening
                  surging of waves   **EROS**
      TETHYS and green under sun
                  desiring the rushing   **EROS**
      TETHYS shearing and joining
                  cuspform and intricate **EROS**
     TETHYS splitting and forming
                  the raptures of growth **EROS**
                  and erosion's spirit
                  apart, the pangs   **EROS**
                  of yearning completion
                  with the mind of **EROS**

Wanderer

Pied patches of snow lie in the meadows' lees,
in streaks on screes where slides have coursed,
along the ridges' crest in sinusoidal cornices,
in dappling flecks, in lakeside depths,
in windshadows of the snow-tormented trees.
It is late June; the day's solstitial length endures.
Anemones from snowbeds pop up and bloom
and capture light in cups of blossoming,
gathering all the bright infinity of light
unto themselves, their parabolic efficiency reflecting
in white parables, and bursting the breaking day
to stamens and pistils each energumen of light,
transforming it to sweet and honeyed phantasms,
their tossing heads emerging from the snow,
their conserved energy from prior summers surging them
to recapitulate themselves, and toss their reproductive
selves up to the sun in urgent celebration.
Tenacity is nine-tenths of their lives,
countering the tenebrous fact, the gloom,
in a tenuous reglimmering and gathering.
Tenacity and delicacy, the deliberate holding on—
the characteristics of this scrabbling rooting
and florescence in a brief season attract me,
and so among this wild and weathered place
I stop and pause, see saxifrages
in their empurpled bells abruptly bloom
and bear a brimming glimpse of royalty
against plebeian rocks and gravel;
glimpse "rock-breakers" speaking saxon,
small drabas against aridity and dryness
scrabbling skywards, seeking sunlight;
diminutive androsace's delight,
gentility and jasmine in the rock;
on slipping slopes the bright stonecrop,
its leaves like fingers grasping it;
and then among anemones the bracts of paintbrush—
crimson and cerise, magenta and maroon,
pale white and cream, and parasitic,
drawing its sustaining succor from the roots
of all this crazy-quilted carpeting.
The willow forest here is dwarfed;
it is a minute world a majesty of mountains

here imposes on these plants, these orophytes,
this finite web, this frail and fragile,
durable, enduring garden at the heights,
and if I stop to think on it, though giant,
I am just about as small, as slight
as eldritch, dessicated, gnarled, nasty forms
this thin atmosphere and wuther
make from aspiration and yearning to live.
Bold and glacially emblazoned peaks
stretch their grey gauntlets over me,
as though the hands of giants hover here
and could pluck me as casually as could I
pick gems from this bejewelled bright fell;
grey field of crumbling limestone,
lichen-littered rhizocarpic maps of mind;
what space, what place? where do we dwell?
Ourselves we are small flowers seeking sun,
holding this brief bit of flesh, this humous,
humanness, these fluids in a veined vessel
firm against a drying wind, gaunt weather,
the freezing, melting, freezing cycles
of the day as with the world we turn.
Thin skin of clouds like a lamb's fell
wisps in mare's-tails the sky westering
and faint chill fills in tussock hollows;
a glistening droplet on the frail snow freezes,
and refracts in iris, like a clouding cataract,
the fading sun's last rainbow as it gels,
a savage insight; the downy hair bedewed
on the anemones' stems is not fast freezing,
for it insulates itself in feathered fronds;
the sundog waves of bleak light wash the lea,
the frosted tongue of storm begins to lick
the cotyledons of the lilies as sleet sweeps
the crest of the pass in pellet rain
and small hard kernels of harsh snow hop
and skim the boiler-plated pans of remnant snow.
The upland slopes begin to disappear,
the grey of gravel vanishes in clouds' grey space,
and distance dims, diminishes, as chill descends.
As fog clings to my glasses, it smears
the crystalline world that was, just a wink ago,

quite here and quintessentially spring,
and summer's verging imminence is membrane thin,
transparently distilled, deliberately delicate
as this spring boisterousness reveals
the cruel arctic contretemps
of surly and—for here—quite seasonable extreme.
It is a vanished world, for vapours hide
all that I take my bearing by; I must rely
on knowing down will deliver me to darkness
in the shadows of the thicker forest;
there is a sanctuary in the Engelmanns,
but first I must descend through lingering larches,
the mists of green, their small leaves growing,
pass down beside the nodding heads
of dog-toothed violets in lily shells,
the scum of rusty needles on the snowpatch,
and wonder why I should have thought the meadows
were beneficent in June's bright bounty.
Black-green, the glowering spruces ghost themselves
from out the swirling ecstasy of storm,
and thunder starts to rumble and rebound
in all the fogbound, deep-grudging cloud
that misery has made of all that was magnificient.
Where are you, Wordsworth? Should I wait this out?
Is there some force here I should face,
so frightening and forbidding it conceals
itself behind this mask of torment,
while it dares to speak in syllables of storm?
Clouds rag, wind rages, the day torments itself,
and there is reminder here: the world's not cruel.
On the narrow, plant-nestling plateau is life,
persistent, sustaining, surviving, vibrant life,
and on the Earth's thin skin, in thinning air,
in summer's scherzos played against the tympani,
it will suffice, will succor, will wear.
It is not lonely here; it is alone;
it's part, apart; it's apprehended summer
with the savage teeth of winter always near.
It is a visceral reminder of how thin an atmosphere
we always breathe, how tenuous life always is,
and how from barren places beauty springs in storm.
The greyed-down blackness on the solstice

is not comfort, yet the green through greyness,
slurried snow, the windworn heathered scarps,
the bleakness, barrens, wars of weather
seems here to sing assuredly, to flourish,
be a banner flown more bravely in flamboyance
than all the lusher gardens of the lower places.
Deep draughts of air I draw into my lungs,
my nostrils sting, chill chafes my cheeks;
I do not hesitate to watch, but hurry hence
to sheltering forest; and then, beneath the boughs
of ancient trees I stop, I lurch myself beneath them,
and in the tumult and the din, I glory
in the thrones of thunderheads about.

Ranging

Range is limit is depth is height is near is far is close is range
is is
travel mountains
is is
roam peaks
is is
wander summits
is is
saunter crags
is is
amble heights
is is
sojourn parallels
is is
variation totality
is is
distance sweeping
is is
rank limitation
is is
rove fields
is is
vary pasture
is is
line meadow
is is
graze tors
is is
difference how
is to
row find
is is
range is location is place is stove is here is it is spot is range

Range   is   limit   is   depth   is   height   is   near   is   far   is   close   is   range
is   is
travel   mountains
is   is
roam   peaks
is   is
wander   summits
is   is
saunter   crags
is   is
amble   heights
is   is
sojourn   parallels
is   is
variation   totality
is   is
distance   sweeping
is   is
rank   limitation
is   is
rove   fields
is   is
vary   pasture
is   is
line   meadow
is   is
graze   tors
is   is
difference   how
is   to
row   find
is   is
range   is   location   is   place   is   stove   is   here   is   it   is   spot   is   range

utterance

collision

tangle   impact

vocable

subsidence

temper

slickensides   *dance*

shore

plates

time   frenzy

fatigue

fury   *fold*

friability

seams

agony   spring   *slip*

bending   faulting

erosion

weariness   **abrasion**

frangibility   *wear*

mangle

stress   adhesion

cluster

silt

settling

fluvium

borne   *alluvium*

conglomeration   muck

bones   exoskeleton

flow   magma   *plume*   **water**

storm   **majesty**   *fume*   aqueou

stridency   *silence*   jocosity

wave   **melancholy**

flume

trump

blackness

terror   **fear**

motion   endless   pity

The fields

our minds

moving back

our minds

at play

and forth

wander in

scattering

discovering

disparate

combinant

facts

cloven

conglomerate

and fictive

places

alluvia

appearances

from high

to deep

despair

to low

and shallow

paradise

and back

sediments

the world

the ranks

arrayed

aging

files of

in strata

revealing

peaks

displaying

their age

how far

parallel

their form

how near

and reaching

composing

how clear

north

structure

the imagination

by west

the eye

fills in

and south

ranges

the bare perceived

by east

eyes range

mountains

the distant

blue

fields

afar

fading

selfdom

and far

away

Scan sky ridge
seek one source
path bright leading

pulse dawn pink
following brim toward
pulsing ringing bowl

we make what we make
of what we see our own
is not we are reality

all we read experienced
information we sense in time
gathers our pasts beyond

into a welded unity
totality into the search
entire presence enduring

eagles the wanderer the fells
bearing toward desire
snow forest atonement

the ring of peaks the peaks
the whiteness of light of ecstasy
of glaciers of dread scanning

Weathering time's ravaging
and revelation the wear and wearing
exposure of nakedness and flesh

wondering how long we waited
for the world's intelligence infusing
part of it to accept

our unremittingly and assuredly
wondering how long beauty
in the world awaited us to behold truth

fossils crinoid stems
are made of harder rock
weathering exposes the fronds

shows age rages
storms shallow sea the wind
moving in waves the water

the shells the clothing burdening
the bare stone exposes
and new storms wear erosion

and winter seems
always to burden the world
with storm weathering

```
Finding how far          far
away our eyes            eyes
make motes immense       immensity
connects what's seen     seen
to how we see it         it
how we see's             sees
a part of                of
seeking                  seeking
source                   source
                         the ear                 ear
                         can hear                hear
                         and distinguish         distinguish
                         whisper                 whisper
                         in turbine              turbine
                         differences of          of
                         turbine and turban      turban
                         thunder                 thunder
                         asunder and as under    under
                         thunder the clouds      clouds
                         loud susurration        susurration
                         crackles                crackles
                         a moment before         before
                         the thunder             thunder
                         cracks and              and
                         the rain falling        falling
                         as bolt cleaves         cleaves
                         from cloud and          and
                         cloud spalls            spalls
and                                              and voice
feelings                                         feelings
as                                               as they spring
sought                                           sought
in                                               in all the wondering
world                                            world surrounding
parts                                            parts of world
sought                                           sought everywhere
```

(we add as we subtract; taking from, we provide; and what we cannot be
(we are for others, proliferating richness, profligate spenders;
(as the river the land removes, the land removed is valley;
(nor is there way for removal to occur until there's source.)

Wanderer II

Wherever I wander   —in valley, on fell—
I bear in my bedroll   a burden of memory
confounding my comfort,   confusing my dreams,
thwarting my footfall   in heath and in hinterland:
do from the forests' tongues   murmurings' meanings
emerge to embodiment   emboldened in bear?
do   from my breathing,   smokily misting,
vapourize semblances   of smoke round a spit?
Deep-shadowed to cliff crest,   upright and abrupt,
canyon encloses   my wayfaring spirit
that sun seeks,   that warmth wants,
companionship craves   in the wan world
deep snow's created   in the cleft Earth.
Whiskyjacks glide   softly and silently
from fir bough to fir bough,   watching me trudge
the soft snow on snowshoes   up from the chasm;
the last light,   the glistening gold
of oblique shafts,   catches cliff crest
while forlorn I wander   in darkness and shadow,
at day's end   enduring the world's weight,
my legs' agony,   the darkling despair
of ignorance,   of not knowing whither
my route lies to passwards,   to prospect of esctasy,
or to thickets of deadfall,   the forests of dread.
Is it   rest   or fretfulness in the frost
awaits me,   this long night of lingering
in which I cannot rest,   must relentlessly
persist and endure   if I'm to persevere.
Dark blue, imbued with indigo,   the snow
is all and only what there is   ahead of me—
no jagged trees in clumps   no shadows now,
a dome of snow glowing palely,   ghostly snow
without tracks my tread breaks   as I trudge.
It is all stillness,   stillness and silence
except for the crunch,   the crackle of footfall,
and sometimes on willows   the crust wallows
and I collapse   but must drag myself up.
At the solstice I started   this journey northwards,
the shortest of days,   the darkest of dusks,
the onset of winter,   bleakness and blackness
around me like memories   blurring in tiredness:
the grey-smeared sky,   the sea-washed wharf,

the words of my father,   foretelling my fate—
". . . send you to Australia,"   the end of his tirade,
but I said, "Not Australia,   that's for your convicts;
"I'd like to go to Canada."   "If that be your choice . . ."
And so, banished to Banff,   here I made home,
forgetting my promise   to a lass in Liverpool
I'd be back in a year;   her yearning eyes
I still can see,   and that was five years ago.
Where is she now?   Nestled in comfort
while whiteness, night   and the prospect of the pass
are all that is left to me   in this great loneliness?
Is this the last of the lakes   this flatness
I'm crossing?   Ah, there rises the ridge
I must cross: and the crenellate palisade.
Then, when I stop   to boil tea in my billy,
awaiting the water   to melt from the snow,
the first mist and large flakes   fall from the morning
and the forest's far margins   vanish in veils,
and I exhort the fire,   "Hurry up, damn you, boil,
"We've got miles to make.   Quit your damned sputtering;
"Sizzle it down."   My eyes scan the slopes
the gauze of the storm   is starting to fog.
Uncertainty seizes me: I know not
precisely the way,   the passes, the valleys,
the creek run that leads   up the long valley;
and without the summits   as guideposts, as guardposts,
I cannot pace my progress   nor sleep with assurance.
I wonder if whether   he remembers my promise
to bring up a bottle   and share it at dinner
on New Year's   there where he winters his horses
three days or four or more   north of the railway;
and it all starts to take on   the temper of tumult
for, be he not home   when I reach there,
I'll have carried this bottle   through blizzard
stupidly, stuporously   drink myself
rotten with rum   and set up the bottle
as calling card   and depart otherwise unannounced.
Hunched now and huddling   my body about me,
I watch the clumps of snow   collapsing, melting
and hold my chill hands   to the flickering flames
and add more snow   to the pile in the pot,
and survey the thickening storm   swarming the trees,

60

the greying-down light   the lost luminescence,
the furred-out, the fraying   spars of Engelmann spruce,
and, gladdened by steam   wisping and withering out
from the pan,   I tear up more twigs
and enliven the fire,   my fingers in coatflap
seeking the canister   my tea's in.
"Coot-crazy, cold-crazed idiot,"   I mutter,
"you've got to be crazy;   this place has dislodged you;
"you can't see where you've come from,   you can't tell
"where you're going;   and the mad mist is masking
"the ghastly shapes   of the mountains.
"Why don't you turn back?   The bottle for Tom
"is only a premise,   not really a promise."
As wind swoops round the tree   I swallow my tea,
torture my toes in my moccasins   back into feeling,
strap on the snowshoes   and start again
up the slope,   the white mist around me,
my body bent to its task,   my thighs tightening,
a band of frost   clenching my face
and nips of wind   biting my brow,
trying to keep the vale's dip,   the depression
to my left as I veer   to the valley's long axis
and head my way   into wind walking,
flinching the flex   into my toes,
and arguing,   —over the pass and beyond,
the wind will diminish   when I'm in the trees;
but for now I must struggle,   stay walking,
persist in the struggle,   ward off weariness.
Can I grant myself rest   at the pass and the place?
Farewell to family,   the dockside departure,
and who could have known   how hither I'd wander
here among mountains,   eager and keening?
At whiles I wish   I could make of this waywardness
a pain and a punishment   worthy of banishment;
let them I have left   be sorrowful and sober.
How could they know here   would be so much beauty
even in meagreness,   famine and freezing
that I feel I've been cast out   to richness, reward,
to a country sufficiently wild   for my wandering?
It is suddenly moonflood,   the fully flung disc
of pale gold that glints   on the gauntness of fell;
Orion is rising,   and now it's with ease

I'm descending,   the great hunter hovering
over my waywardness,   under his watchful eye.
Ah, would that my weariness   were less upon me,
I'd stay here and survey   this solemn landscape,
but there in the flanked firs   I must sleep.
Let fretfulness flame   this fury, this folly;
let dreams descend   on this body, this burden:
I'll eat and I'll drink;   I'll sleep and I'll dream,
and at dawn   my wearying muscles will mount
on these snowshoes again,   and I'll walk as I choose
bearing this bottle of rum   and surprise him,
no doubt, when I knock   at his door,
for he'll have forgotten   my promise.

Letter to Mary Townsend Sharples Schäffer Warren

"You couldn't ask for quieter neighbours,"
you used to tell my mother,
speaking of the graveyard's citizens
across Learn's Hill from your place, Tarry-a-While.
I find myself more frequently looking for their addresses
and yours, as if to post them letters, tell them things,
account for what we're doing day to day and year to year.
Accounting or recounting? I read the other day
accounting goes the other way: we borrow from the Earth
our children's use of it. I think you'd understand.
You gave us better than we're handing on, I think,
but we are learning, albeit slowly.
You'd be surprised to see what's being made of you:
a book, a reprint of your **Old Indian Trails** we made anew
with colour reproductions of the lantern slides
you so long ago quite lavishly hand-coloured,
appended with your heretofore unpublished text
about the mapping and the exploration of Chaba Imne;
an exhibition of your works with large-size photos
Ed derived by Cibachrome from those same lantern slides;
and there is talk of turning you into a movie,
the babble of the brook of gossip suggesting
who better could be found than Jane Fonda
to play your robust, quite intriguing self;
your self the shells of myth are circling wider,
and you start to grow, expand, become a wider set
of meanings, markings, unlimitations;
it may be what you thought you'd like to be
when you suggested you were on the subject
of these mountains an encyclopaedia.
Sometimes I wonder about the hedges on your yard:
the imposition of a sense of order
on untrammeled nature, the hedges are so alien
to everything you came to love by what you meant
when you said "garden."

My Garden,
you declared,
is neither raked nor hoed.
It has no signs prohibiting loitering;
sprinkler and fertilizer are alien to it;
it juxtaposes   colours   in combinations
the eyes of horticulturalists would
consider   madness.

It is an
ordered wildness.

Pasque Flowers and Spring Beauty,
nodding blues of the campanulates,
the tiny orchids, Fly-spotted, Coral Root,
the shyly tonsured Drummond's Dryas,
the brilliant orange of Western Wood Lilies,
small flaming Shooting Stars,
the slippers of Calypso stepping,
the greyish-yellow of Wolfwillow blooms,

an ordered wildness

in
contradistinction to
your parrot's
wild disorderedness in
reciting, "Where, o where has my little dog gone"
"Go on! Go on!"
which he, of course, added on.

I like to think of your splendid jest, so happily played out
upon your eastern relatives who so much wanted, sans effort,
to emulate your summers on the trail,
and so you gave them a pack trip three days long
that took them deep into the mountains.
A whole morning of preparing, watching wranglers, packers getting ready,
tying diamond hitches, heaving loads,
and fitting out the dudes with boots and chaps and hats,
before the line of horses sauntered slowly from the stable,
easing   up   the road toward the big hotel and past it,
then cut down through pine forest **off the trail**,
and having on occasion to spur their horses over deadfall,
duck sweeping branches, they all loved it.
By the river they stopped to check the ford
before their guide decided it was safe
and plunged his horse into the boiling current.
It took the afternoon to get them all across,
and then they rode downstream and turned the mountain's corner
while their guide looked carefully about to find a place for camp.
The following day, an hour wasted searching for the horses,
they had to cross the river by an island
and then rode a glacially deposited ridge beside the strange formations,
picked out a safe way to descend and crossed the railroad tracks
and made their way quite carefully along a creek
and to a lake where they made camp
and praised their lucky stars how fortunate they were.
On their third morning, fully in their confidence,
they made their preparations rapidly;
their guide had warned them it was miles they had to go
to get to Banff.
And so it was near dusk and twenty miles later
the pack string wearily approached the barns,
and none of your relatives the wiser
they had never been more than six or seven miles from town,
the horses spent their first night near the stable,
and the wranglers drank their nights away in Banff.
The only difficulty Warren had
was to keep from laughing and to try to make it seem so difficult.

I wonder what you'd think to see it all now opened up,
to cars, to casual visitors who wonder whether
they can make it up to Jasper and back in a day,
when scarce six weeks were adequate for you and Mollie.
They'll not accept the country was far better known
by you and your kind then, when the century began;
and it takes time to get to know anywhere quite well.

The less that's known of it, the better it can be known.
Those relatives who took the three days' packtrip around Tunnel
perceived it slowly and carefully, and knew the force of rivers
ere they were done, or else they had not gone.

Not that you would have complained about the roads too much:
you would have been the first to open up the windscreen,
to see and feel the wind fierce in your eyes
as you and Mary did when with her brothers
you came to the Rockies, riding on the boxcar roof
all the way from Morley up to Laggan.
(Did you ever apologize to William Twin
(for having him drive horses all the way up there
(so you could ride those last few miles, Laggan up to Lake Louise?)
There's just a jot of "Greenhorn!" in your relating
how uncomfortable it was to sleep on spruce bough beds
that first night in the wilderness
and vowing that you'd never sleep beneath the stars again.
Great irony that "Mary Schäffer," Philadelphian,
in later summers spent seasons on the trail,
regretting only "Civilisation and its Discontents"
eventually would replace the idylls of the quest.

George Fox felt God's grandeur quivering in himself,
but did not disavow the world therefore,
and knew subjective wilderness could reward;
a pre-Romantic notion of an Eden in America,
the prelapsarian wild Edward Hicks evoked
in gentle wilds where lion and lamb lay side by side;
how Peaceable a Kingdom.

If anything's to be made from Quaker thought
and how you came to be "a hunter of peace"
where cougar, grizzly, moose, and ram
in nature's equilibrium assort themselves,
then is it "The Peaceable Kingdom" thee was in seach of?
Did, when the Endless Chain seemed to seek infinity,
thee contemplate its orderedness?
Awareness is a human trait,
like laughing, blushing, weeping,
and it seems to sire them
as it does awe, respect, and contemplation, sense of loss,
the ranged meanings we—and thee—ascribe
to wilderness and lives examined,
"endless chain"?

Inner light
radiant suffusion

illuminating   darkness
words   blanketing
telling   everything
tolling   lives

Panther Falls
Ka-toon-da Tinda

windy   plains

Chaba Imne

the rapture

the ecstasy

Thy husband died, and thee was left alone;
his botany unfinished thee took up, completed, published;
then, forsaking warnings, thee departed for the north,
the barely-sought-out trails of ranges north from Laggan,

hunting peace

only in the high places

were he   and thee

together

Epeirogeny

Learning the world spins, I wondered why
        it did not fling us off,
Episode   the older of my brothers having demonstrated
        with the hand-cranked gramophone the nature of the force
by placing aggies on the turntable and easing in the clutch.
(Harold argued from his august eight,
(it was the spinning somehow held us in
(by filling up a bucket almost full
(and twirling while he held it in both hands.
      (I thought he demonstrated that the earth was somehow retroflexive,
      (the Earth containing at its core the flaming sun.
      (His argument he was the sun
      (demonstrably held less water than the bucket.)

Learning the world spins, I hoped it possible
        I could be free of it by leaping up,
Epifocus   by leaping high enough to watch the world run widdershins
        while I would land a somewhere else
a league or more away, and thus by leaps and hopes and hops
I'd circumnavigate the globe till I got home.

Elaborate conceits availed themselves
to bolster hoped-for tropes of global travel:
the earnest naive David Douglas notion we all have had
of coming home from opposite the way we went.

I stationed kids to watch me run away,
although I would not hope for hopping leaps,
private tests having demonstrated—even on the park's big swings—
I lacked the oomph to elevate myself enough to stay aloft
a long enough to let the Earth's enantiodromia reveal itself.
I told them by a periphrastic mumble
I'd circumnavigate the circumgyrate twirling ball of Earth and
—not pausing long enough to explicate my crossing of the oceans—
starting eastward, I would arrive *circumbendibus*
ten minutes later from the western edge of town.
By their circumspective nods they gave their doubts away.

It was elusiveness that led me through the woods
      (audacious proof that thrust my stomach up my neck,
      (requiring that I swallow all my fears of bears)
and when I had returned they all were gone.

Still I hoped that running broad jumps were a way
that track stars had of leaping high enough
the world slipped out from under them.

The like inquisitive curiosity led me to wonder
                    where a kid like me could buy a magic carpet;
Epicrisis   since science failed me, I'd resort to arcane arts.
                    Mother told me Mrs Round (I'm not making this up;
(her name was Elsie Round; it had been Elsie Squayre),
who owned the Odd Craft Shop, might carry them,
in the back room tucked away
behind the racks that held the Thornton W. Burgess books
I had by then read most of
(for I was on to Sinbad, rocs, Ali Baba, and Aladdin;
(and Scheherezade's albeit-bowdlerized stories
(fascinated me more than Old Mother West Wind's tales).

After lunch I left at five past one
to stop en route at Mrs Round's
and ask her were I to save my pennies, nickels, dimes
from my allowance,
might I purchase one.
"I'm awfully sorry, Jonny," quoth Mrs Round
as she peered over her glasses to look me in the eye,
"I'm awfully sorry, but I haven't any flying carpets
"in my stock just now. They are becoming scarce.
"But I will let you know should one come in."

" . . . Should one come in'" she'd said.
                    I scarce believed my luck.
Epiphora   *"How much would just a small one cost?"* I must have asked.
                    She wasn't sure,
but not beyond the means of one who really wanted . . . .

I floated on to Miss Brown's classroom,
getting there with just scant seconds before the classes started,
and had to wait till recess to tell the other kids
I had first dibs on Mrs Round's next flying carpet,
having to explain how wonderful a magic carpet was
and what it did
and how it worked.

I think she must have told me, or I'd read,
how difficult they are to manage,
to make the carpet do as it was told
and how I might not get to make it work 'til I was older.
Wise of her to be so cautious.

I must have asked her two or three times more at two-week intervals
          if she had heard from Persia or Baghdad.
Epigee   She told me only I should keep on hoping.
          I kept on hoping.
I'd sit cross-legged and my hands upon my knees
in what I thought a pasha fashion ought to be,
turbaning my brow in pasha passion,
sitting on the little carpet in the bedroom
that in its interstitial indigo and blood red pattern
intimated Araby,
and close my eyes
and wish
and wish
and misperceive my silent muscles' spasms
as the tug of mind to what could matter,
and hope to levitate myself and it
'til I should feel the ceiling tap my head.
It never happened.
(Was that the year that Bubby and the Mount-Teen Club
(performed *Aladdin?* Louis Worthington and Ted Stafford
(in a comic camel by the name of Nuphsed?   Nuphsed.)
Santa Claus by then had metamorphosed into myth,
         But Sammy Ward assured me with a twinkling eye
Epiphenomenon   he'd seen a magic carpet once in India,
         and told me of another thing more wonderful
he'd seen while he was there:

      "It were in Bombay.
      "in a bazaa' there,
      "we 'eared a feller playing flute and follered
      "through the mazy alleyz 'til we found 'im
      "and zeen him zwaying back and forth and zlowly
      "oop the lid from orf 'iz bazket moved,
      "and oop it zidled, did 'iz rope
      "az though it were a znake alive,
      "and 'eld thar in the air, joost like a worm,

"and then 'e put 'iz flute bezide
"and told 'iz lad to climb it, oop the rope;
"which 'e did, egzept 'e 'ezitated at the top
"and zhouted down in 'eathen tongue
" 'e'd go no further.
"Zo the feller took 'iz zord and brandished it,
"and zhure enough 'iz lad went further oop and dizappeared.
"It were a mozt myzteriouz thing."

To prove a magic by another magic
did not seem dubious at all.

"Then 'e called 'im to coome back down again,
"and we 'eared zhouting, 'No! No!'
"Zo then 'e grips 'iz zord between 'iz teeth
"and climbz 'iz rope and zhoutz again.
"We 'ear 'iz lad zhout back.
"Zo then 'e zwingz 'iz zord oop in the air
"and all the zhouting oot of air iz zilent
"Zo 'e climbz back down,
"picks oop 'iz flute
"and ztartz to play again.
"Iz rope beginz to zway and zidle in the air
"and zlowly fall back down and coil into 'iz bazket;
"and then 'e takez the lid
"and plazez it atop 'iz bazket joost like that.
"Zoodenly we 'eared a zhouting moofled-like
"and from the bazket ztepz 'iz lad entire again.
"It were a mozt remarkable event,
"and I zhould like to zee it 'appen once again
"to tell me that me eyez 'ad never told me lie."

His telling was so real it kindled faith.

Sammy was a carpenter from London who affected Yorkshire on occasion
but retreated to his Cockney for his tales of Albert and the Lion,
or other Ramsbottom recounts.

Were there such magic as he told of,
surely I could find a flying carpet.
In all my delitescent fantasies I read of more vehicular phenomena.

Were Mrs Round not sure
(for she was speaking now of "years" instead of weeks)
I'd find another way.
Now I had heard of "Seven-League Boots"
and they replaced my fading hope
of ever getting Mrs Round to say just when
I might expect my carpet to come in
with the hope the other kids had quite forgotten too
                         my erstwhile hope of getting one, of owning one,
Epiphonema   with the hope of yet another hope,
                         a hoped-for hope of boots
to bear their wearer in one pace full seven leagues.
I knew by then better than to ask my mother once again
where they might be for sale, but asked her, sneakily,
just how far a league might be,
and she supposed it was about as far as Anthracite,
and wondered why I'd want to know a thing like that.

                    (I've looked it up:
                    (a league can vary from a distance of 2.42 statute miles
                    (up to 4.6,
                    (reckoned usually at somewhere nearabouts 3,
                    (which means that Mother was nearabout correct.
                    (How did she know a thing like that?)

McCaffrey's was the place for shoes,
for Dubbin, Black Cat polish, shoe repairs,
for leather straps and laces,
and it smelt of tanners' oak,
of richly warm and acrid odours,
cobblers' thoughts,
Morocco, neat's-foot, tannin, gall, and sumac,
exotic places that McCaffrey's craft had cosened.

I know I knew not quite what I expected:
something like a pair of ammonites
with toes like hops that would unfurl to seek far hills
and tow me somehow swiftly in their lee,
or winklepickers with a self-propelling sole,
or Slinkies fastened to a geta-bridge,
or daddy-long-legs coils to spring like Zoomerangs from out the heels.
But Mr McCaffrey said he didn't know what I was speaking of.

How could I know we do not have to jump to move?

By staying in one place we move in slow and elegant pavannes
                    as continents raft slowly on the globe,
Epeirogenic   and where we might have been is somewhere else
                    and where we are is just the carpet longing
for the tugs and yearns of everything to be somewhere else.

        We watch the exoskeletons of sea creatures confetti down,
        like ash, like dust, like time itself,
        to massive banks of quartzite, settling down, becalming,

We write in sand, our language grows,
And, like the tide, our work o'erflows.

Edmund Waller 1606-1687

Is oldest most recent, youngest deepest, or is most ancient
when from the fact of surfaces we scrape away the heaped
a younger or an older past, a presence once a present,
past in present always present, epiphanies of presence
more since time's eroded it, sun and rain and frost,
fractured, furrowed, folded and worn away, it shows
strains that mind developing through species finds deepest hidden?
beyond the faults, the erosion, the bearing away detritus, exposing
the settling down, the sediments of the remote, we reveal omnipresence
amphisbaenic or anisotropic tugs to upwardness, a revelation's omen,
gravity, the rheotropic force of forming fish, and looks its age, lined
the yearning of the struggle of the spine to the recently developed
be a central nervous system, to be bilateral, and inbred intelligence
oneself upon oneself or in genetic opposition, of all accumulated sense,
is not a fault, a cosmic slip on some banana my sediments exactly, or
is a jest of Earth's morphology, a clap the downward acquiescence to
must give, capitulate or otherwise escape the wish to seek the sun,
the flight of monoclinal single-celled stand erect, to be the bole of man,
will to upwardness and even—or uneven to be symmetrical, and to reflect
and slip—cataclysm in orogenic ecstasy, to be split and seek unity
while the slow coalescence of crustal on which we've slipped or spilled
tremors rumble the temporal upward of agony as under pressure surfaces
lead to the breakers on the shore by enantiodromia, epeirogeny,
it yearns, it fractures and slides spirits'— within their walls—
are the interface, the slickensides rocks capitulate, break, burgeon
the urge to live, to grow, to form the slow rolling, the heat forcing
to find a form and force a path structures and the deep emergent
to make of hope dream, to climb and recumbent pliability of rocks
and splay legs on sand, slip those are the breaks it yields as
breathe, cough, dry out, fade, time against time until confusions
beat fins on rocks, and try of dip and strike reveal the force,
the sun could give, seek love from acids and the protoplasmic soup,
up from the inchoate, the barely-shaped,
the world's well walls up to the brimming rim
and stumble, draw hot air into gills, expunge,
slide back into the brine, the swelling sea,
again to sense what shadow meant, what share
in torrid vapours and desert-blasting wind.

Epigone

*The Professor of Geology
applies Principles of Uniformity
to demonstrate Folding and Faulting
in sedimentary beds:*

our Superficial Supposition
for Collusions and Collisions,
Unconformities and faults abound
structurally investigate the ground
of the Fisticuffs of rock,
may in the Senescent shock,
may in the Termagant show,
from Sedentary Torpors flow,

We should not think that all *perfection, uniformity displayed*
rests on visible Congruous forms, *fault or fold have made,*
Epochs, Ages, Eras, *Sanctimonious Upheaval at the core,*
when we dip deep enough, and *Formation mask the Obstreperous Bore,*
for all the characteristic *overlies the Disputatious Fogs,*
Efficacious—some say Late Clamorous—Bogs
the Tremors of the Adolescent
concealed Vituperous Sediment *Gluttonous tremblings of the Gut,*
and Unctuous Tergiversations *muddling in the Acrimonious Butt;*
the diagram of temporal ordering arrays *when Amorous Erections likely chance,*
conceals the interruptions plume or passage *Appetites of Subsurficial Dance,*
Sagacious Superimpositions hide the *Abstemious may flow in Glamorous Extrusions,*
Intrusions of the Platitudinous *Disturbances of bedrock, false conclusions*
the Rapturous Corruption *Discontinuities and obvious Mendacity,*
Vituperous Conniptions confuse the *Late Capricious and Vivacious Capacity*
in the Early Avaricious, the Spacious, Specious, Oracular, Vespertine
Transitions of Voracious Adulterous Formations frequently are seen.
We cannot tell with certainty *the Rapscallion Raptures formed,*
Orogenies of Passion are *in the Concupiscent, as it stormed*
the quiet, dormant *with signs of low Rambunctious ooze,*
Erotic Ambiguities, Eructations, should you choose,
in violent display of *tracks in Late Precocious slime,*
Predacious Occlusions, conclusions out of place and time,
Voluminous **Vexation led to Inconsequential Slack**
Interruptions **Interim, the Omnipresent Graywacke.**

*Cantankerous Eruptions
Rampant Happenstances
Early Adolescent Epoch
Rampageous Ramifications,
Gelatinous Conceptions,
Extemporaneous*
**the Vesuviant
in the Intermiddling**

The ancient river, older than the mountains that it bears
grain by grain to settle and subside within and in the Bearpaw Sea,
flows with its burden still, from range to range declining,
wearing away, shearing away the decomposing and recumbent ranges.
      (In Grade Six Enterprise we studied Egypt for two months;
      (when the precocious kid gave a little talk about the river
      (and its meaning to the Nile Delta dwellers,
      (he suggested the inundation of the flood each year
      (disintegrated the mud-brick huts; Billy A.
      (had the cheeky kid repeat the decadollar word.)

A hundred million years.
Two hundred million years.
A stagnant pool of half a continent's immensity, part of Pangaea,
beneath a sun of zenith height shimmers in the waves of heat.

      Beneath the scowling violence of cloud-tormented thickening sky
      the ribbled blackness of the gorgon swarms in edging swamps:

monstrous bellowing

brontosaurus challenges

of terrible lizards

fanged marginalia

grotesque   awesome spectacle

sundering Earth's soft flesh

sometimes mud swallowing

thunder-clotted

storms of mayhem

and the river

grain   by   grain   and   mile   by   mile   sifts   time   down   around   them

desert

catastrophic tumult

immensity of diet

barkhans of time

wind drift unimaginable

gargoyle-faced fish

ferns of forests

forests of ferns

age does not yield to age   the dragons persist

the inundations

of the sea and grit

the   heaped-up   layers   of   progressive   generations   unto   generations

generating

variant species

fish in the tidal pools

the periwinkles and the coral

the seaweed searching out the land

and giant trees

the sun unblinking

for ages as

boulders and rubble
       the tumbledown
              pile of blocks
the heaped up
       crumbledown
              piled up
babble-scrabble scree
       we descry
              and descrying
describe
       distinguish
              its confusion
it's confusion
       as words from the past
              become morphemes of memory
the tissue-issuance
       of meanings
              we build from blocks toward speech
self
       selving
              selvage
salvage
       salve
              salving
salvation
       solution
              dissolution
dissoluble
       solvable
              solve
and the solving
       and wondering
              if "self"
involves "Solving"?
       soul
              sole
solace
       solus
              sol
solifluction
       helios
              helium

heel
        heal
              soul and heal
Health
        and
              Salvation
or
        is it
              sole and heel
dancing
        merrily
              toward solution
pass
        and passed
              and passed and past
past existence
        or passed existence
              passed by what we judge the past by

The language is crumbledown
        tumbledown
              derelict
hand-me-down ground-down
        ground-up
              finger-clinging clay
pebbles and drubs
        dribbles and dibbles
              dobbles and daubs
gobs and globs
        blobs and blops
              and plops
the gabble-babble
        the globular round tones
              of puddles, muddles and confusions
the ripplings
        ripples
              dipples and dapples
of rain drops
        in middling and meddling
              intermingling and mangling
fandangling
        and dangling
              and coupling

of what we hear
                with what
                        we think we hear
the near-hearing
                mishearing
                        shearing of sounds' sense
and senses' sounds
                until meaning
                        is ground down
to a fine grind
                fine-ground
                        semblance of sounds' intent
(sounds in tent)
                resembling
                        its grounding
to build up
                by accretion
                        of sand, gravel, clay
the sifting down
                shifting up
                        down-settling silt
the sand crystals
                accumulating their weight
                        and their waiting

Look how the river, the forgotten river, river of ancience,
flows through aridity, the planet's once-lifelessness,
bearing the dirt down, wearing the Earth down,
carrying its burden from the great dousing rainstorms,
carrying silts and salts in solution, forming the salt-tasting ocean,
and for aeons the ions, free in the ocean,
the waters, the wave-washing waters, the seacliffs eroding,
collapsing, energumens of carbon, hydrogen, nitrogen
linking and linking, coupling in energy, the rnn-thnn,
drizzling from bonding to bonding

                the fondling
                        the linking-up happening
        of primal
                materials
                        of thinking occurring—

My first kaleidoscope contained a magic of geometry;
no time fled faster than those hours within its cell;
I loved the squaredance of its falling flakes and chips,
the randomness, the insecurity, the beckoning search
for repetition, and the resolution in reflections;
shimmering greens, translucent blues, and shots of blood,
frosted flakes of dust, the patterning continued as it were
the Earth itself I turned and peered into, or looked down on,
kaleidoscope become a telescope, its world within quite magnified,
a better drama than the phosphenes I had learned to make
by rubbing knuckles up against the orbit of my eyes.
One afternoon at play with Billy I chanced upon a pattern
when the myriad chips of pink and red filled up the lens,
and all the emeralds, turquoises and topazes disappeared;
it was the most amazing globe of accident I'd seen,
so with all caution I could summon, holding the scope
as steadily as a hunter beading on his prey,

Epitasis   I summoned Billy. But, in the moment when he placed his eye
up to the tube, and in the silence, I heard a flake fall.
"You should have been more careful." "I was; I was," he said.

Then I told him, after I had seen what it had become,
how it had been: all red, all fire, all hot and burning.
"Oh," he said. "I'll put it back the way it was."
I knew enough by then to know he could not put it back,
and tried to tell him so, but he persisted faithfully.
I had to sit and draw as Billy fidgeted the tube,
and tried to realign the moment that had been,
and placate his approximations of the wonder that had been.
"It's just like snowflakes. They're all different,"
I explained. "You can't put it back the way it was.
"It'll never be the same again. It was an accident,
"the way it was, and how it happened." The mechanic in him
tried to find a way to line up motes and molecules,
the shifting sands and grains of iridescence,
and I had to check the patterns he had reached
at intervals of once a minute, till I grew bored
and suggested something else to do. He was relieved.

I understood his bold persistence. A year before,
while we were driving up to Lake Louise from Banff,
near Eldon we had seen an ancient train,
a diamond stack atop the locomotive,
stress rods on the boxcars, a caboose from Toonerville.
I had believed then—1946 or '47—
were we to realign ourselves with time,
depart from Banff on just the day and just the hour,
the weather right, all of us in the car,
the picnic packed just so, and reach there then,
again that ancient wondrous train would pass through Eldon,
and even now I sometimes hold my breath when we pass there
and hope the decades will evaporate,
the portal through which that memory of years before had slipped
will reappear, and it will be back then,
whenever then could be.

What has all this to do with leaping up
to let the world run wild and widdershins?
It has to do with what we mean by what we say
when we relate how we were then, and where "where" was
in our recalling "how you should have been there."
We cannot reassemble all the moments of a million,
line up the planets or the continents,
or set the weather like a permanent of cyclones
endlessly repeating: there's a glory.
There is no permanence. The wonder is impermanence:
the jewels in kaleidoscopes we cannot realign
persist in memory as crystals of occasion.

Gondwana   breaks   apart
and   shears   under
Laurasia   separates   itself

It   *is*   *dance*
becomes   the   *kinetic*
shifting   *splitting*   *convergence*
fragments   diffractions   *continents*

until
rafts
merge

collide   heap up   **mass**
smash   along a   **verge**
converge   coast   **line**

propelled
by
Earth's
inner
energy
and
in
tumult

crumble   **crush**   raise
buckling   **the beds**   sediments
strata   **upheaval**   in folds
skyward   **monumental**   until

crust
stresses
breaks
faults

ridges   rise
        while   furl
        all
        the
        while
continents   dance   northerly

At land's mouth into the turbulent sea
                    dark is the ancient flood-river pouring,
Epilogue   the silt settling down in beds silently,
                    but the waves relentlessly eroding the shoring
of seacliffs, the waves inscribing their names
in script in contention as silt and sand sifting
await the tremulous storms to quiet; time tames
eventually, and then in their down-drifting
they fall and they shift, and they settle down
darkly and thickly and slowly accumulate,
worms, crinoids, corals and slime, brown
and buried as sand becomes stone under weight
to an even and level, a stratified bier,
and it deepens and deepens year after year.

Some notes and explanations

The ripples begin where I begin; they wash up on that larger circle, the world.

The lot, the neighbourhood, the milieu, the family, the town, the community, the ring of mountains containing the Bow Valley first, then the greater ranges of the Rockies beyond, the national parks of the continental crest: these are the expanding—the receding—horizons of consciousness "Some Fittes and Starts" involves.

One who chooses to write about his neighbourhood should select it carefully. The spirits of ancient Banff (1883-1914) took up residence in our backyard before I was born. I met them before I knew who they were.

Bill Peyto, the Rockies' most illustrious guide and outfitter, built a rough shack on the grounds where the grazing was good and the Bow River was near. His prospecting and packing partner **Jack Sinclair**, a western Australian from Coolgardie, had been an ore seeker in Bulolo, New Guinea, before he reached the Rockies about 1890. Jack's cabin was more substantial and better constructed than Bill's. At the outbreak of the Boer War Bill and Jack flipped a coin to see who would defend the Empire. Bill won the toss, and in South Africa he rode his horse before enemy lines to draw their fire, inducing them to disclose their locations. After the war he returned to Banff, whereupon Jack, who had tended the claim in Bill's absence, decided to seek his fortune in gold fields of the Transvaal. His arrangement with my grandfather resulted in our family's establishment on the property between Bear Street, Lynx Street, and the river. Nextdoor was **Jimmy Simpson**, an English expatriate who "fell in with 'the boys of Banff'", and became a trapper and hunter in his winters, an outfitter and guide in his summers. He also became Banff's first art collector. Jim was no spirit; he was very much alive, a spritely seventy or so, when I was a kid. **Tom Wilson**, a man from Barrie, Ontario, who had arrived with the railroad survey crews in 1881, and stayed behind in Banff to become the first entrepreneurial spirit engaged in outfitting pilgrims, was Jim's first employer.

Mrs Simpson, very Scottish, was a constant source of oatcakes and Caledonian heritage. She was at the centre of artistic life in Banff, involved in theatre and reading circles, vigourously engaged in figure skating. (The Simpson daughters, Margaret and Mary, had a world career in skating in the 1930s.)

Across the street were two embodied fantasies. **Ike Mills' Riding School** was the ostentatious name of a horse rental stable where the remittance man from Robin Hood Bay swaggered and staggered in practical-joking manner. Once a world champion dogracer, a master of masquerade, Ike was terror incarnate and fascination. Ike's persistent threat, frequently realized, was to headfirst a kid into the manure box, then order him home to tell his mother he needed a bath. **Alma Mills** was a delicate New Englander with French Canadian roots who had been a 'cellist in a ladies' trio which performed at the Banff Springs Hotel where she met and fell in love with Ike. Alma served me my first glass of beer when I was about five. She kept chickens. Next to Ike's was the government building where each morning labourers assembled. Inside the building was an inferno of scattering sparks, **Steve Hope's** smithy shop.

In the family were **Bubby** (Barbara), **Dave**, and **Harold**, my sister and brothers. Up the hill—an ancient bank of the Bow River, truth to tell—beyond the cave Dave and Harold dug in the sandy soil with **Dietz**, a neighbourhood kid, and others, was *Mom's* my paternal grandmother's residence. *Mom* and *Papa*, **Dave White**, married in the last year of Victoria's reign. Their home was a darkness of Victorian bric-à-brac, glass lampshades, tasseled curtains, feather pictures and figurines. Mom's father was **John Donaldson Curren**, a Scottish Presbyterian coal seeker and coal miner. He died a year to the day before I was born: I am ultimately named for him. (*Jon* without an *h*, *Whyte* rather than *White*; a later volume of *The Fells of Brightness* may explain these anomalies.) John Curren is now esteemed as an early naive painter of Rocky Mountain historical subjects and landscapes, their spanking green forests summoning a Rocky Mountain Eden.

Of uncles who lived nearby, **Clifford**, the oldest, married **Mildred**, and they had three sons, **Cliff**, **Donald**, and **Peter**. **Peter**, the nextborn, married **Catharine Robb**, and they became *Pete'n'Catharine*, living a hundred yards north of us in a log house, another source of cookies, meringues, ginger ale and grapefruit juice, conversation and the best library in town. They met at art school in Boston and were painters of portraits and landscapes. **Lila**, the aunt, married **Cameron Stockand**, and they lived in the neighbourhood with their kids until I was four.

Between our house and *Pete'n'Catharine's* was my grandfather's old carriage shed where **Perella** had her stall. In the late 1940s it became *Sammy's Shop*, where **Sam Ward**, an irrepressible tease, a master carpenter, a constant entertainer, was willing to suffer the interruptions of an inquisitive little kid.

It was a well-chosen neighbourhood.

A few other names: **Bill Peyto** packed for **Walter D. Wilcox** in the 1890s. (Marianne Moore quotes Mr Wilcox on Bill Peyto in "An Octopus". Her poem showed me the breadth of subject matter my neighbourhood could encompass.) Mr Wilcox and his friend **Samuel E.S. Allen** explored the Lake Louise region in 1893-1894. Mr Wilcox was a superior photographer. Mr Allen was a linguist and spirited climber. The better namer, Samuel Allen fell into dementia praecox shortly after his summer of joy in the Rockies in 1894; the affliction forestalled his defense of his toponomy on the summit crest of the Rockies; hence Walter Wilcox's names adorn most of the features they competitively named.

The **Vauxes** were dedicated Victorian visitors. Photographers, Philadephians, Quakers, amateur glaciologists, the brothers **William** and **George**, and their sister **Mary**, visited the Rockies first in 1887; their descendents still consider the Rockies and the Selkirks a playground for wildland recreation and intellectual and artistic pursuit. Mary Vaux's teenage friend **Mary Sharples** was a wildflower painter and photographer. Twice married, her first husband, **Charles Schäffer**, was kin of my maternal grandmother. In 1931 my mother visited her *Aunt Mary* and her second husband, **Billy Warren**, in Banff, where she met my father. Mary Sharples Schäffer Warren was Banff's first resident writer. **Dr Charles Fay**, a major early climber in the Rockies and Selkirks, is so distant a relative his kinship is of less importance than his prose which, in *Appalachia*, recounts so much of the history of early alpinism in the Rockies.